MAJOLICA POTTERY

By Mariann K. Marks

COLLECTOR BOOKS
A Division of Schroeder Publishing Co., Inc.

The current values in this book should be used only as a guide. They are not intended to set prices which vary from one section of the country to another. Auction prices as well as dealer prices vary greatly and are affected by conditions as well as demand. Neither the Author nor the Publisher assumes responsibility for any losses that might be incurred as a result of consulting this guide.

Additional copies of this book may be ordered from:

COLLECTOR BOOKS
P.O. Box 3009
Paducah, Kentucky 42001

$9.95 plus $1.00 for postage and handling
Copyright Mariann K. Marks 1983
ISBN: 0-89145-219-2

Printed by Taylor Publishing Company
Dallas, Texas

To my husband Edward O. C. Marks who proposed the original idea for this book and supported, encouraged and assisted me in every way possible during its preparation.

ACKNOWLEDGMENTS

I especially wish to thank my parents, Alice B. and Robert W. Katz, Sr., for their constant support in all my endeavors and for their interest and encouragement in this undertaking.

My sincerest thanks are also extended to the following persons who graciously offered to allow me to photograph their collections or contributed in some special way to the completion of this book.

Tamara Marks
Robert W. Katz, Jr.
James E. Katz
Linda and Steve Horn
Chris Horn
Charles Rebert
Gordon Weniger
Isabelle Flax
Helene Rabin
Tony Antene
Marc Polo
Florence Michalek
Eugene Kosche and The Bennington Museum

INTRODUCTION

Welcome to the wonderful world of majolica where cauliflowers turn into teapots, fans become ice cream dishes, pickles are served from begonia leaves and sugar is spooned from a pineapple. At one time collectors of this colorful and whimsical Victorian pottery were few and far between but today there are many who faithfully attend antique shows, follow the antique shop trail, and sit out endless auctions in search of this brightly colored lead glazed earthenware pottery produced by our ancestors.

There is an immense personal satisfaction to be enjoyed in the building of a collection no matter what its size or the extent of one's personal resources. Some dedicated collectors have flown the world over in search of majolica and never miss an opportunity to continue the hunt. Others search out additions to their collections at local flea markets and small antique shows. Some confine their purchases to mail order sources or through attendance at local and distant auctions. No matter what the source or the funds expended in the search, the ultimate outcome is the same — the pleasure and inner satisfaction that comes from the collection. The truly dedicated collector loves it all; the search, purchase, carting it home, cleaning, labeling, cataloging, researching, and deciding on the proper display spot for each new addition.

The same Majolica that we collect today (related in name only to the 14th century Italian and Spanish ware) was loved and avidly collected by the people who lived during the time of its production. We can only envision our ancestors going shopping in our countries' large department stores and small shops to view the latest offerings of plates, platters, teasets and pitchers from the world's many majolica potters.

In our country the largest producers included Edwin Bennett of Baltimore, Maryland; James Carr, an Englishman transplanted to New York City, of the New York City Pottery Co.; James Scollay Taft who founded the Hampshire Pottery in Keene, New Hampshire; George Morley of Wellsville and East Liverpool, Ohio; the giant's of the industry located in my own home state, Griffin, Smith & Hill, Phoenixville, Pennsylvania; David Francis Haynes, founder of the Chesapeake Pottery Company, producer of the popular Clifton Decor line; Charles Reynolds of the New Milford Pottery Company, New Milford, Connecticut; and a group of potters situated in Trenton, New Jersey, an area which was to become known as the "Staffordshire of America" and included the well known Eureka Pottery Company.

Much less is known about our potters' competitors on the other side of the Atlantic but it is known that much Majolica was produced by Wedgwood, Minton, Copeland, Fielding, and George Jones, thanks to the beautifully marked specimens which delight today's collectors. The diamond shaped English Registry mark found on the bottom of some pieces has revealed work by additional potters such as Shorter & Boulton, Stoke; Banks & Thorley, Hanley; Wardle & Co., Hanley; John Rose & Co., Coalport; and J. Bevington, Hanley, who produced an astounding tail-feather pouring swan pitcher.

In other parts of the world the French contributed many intricate figural pieces. They are known for an incredible array of collectible mouth-pouring pitchers and interesting art nouveau and art deco designs. Some of these pieces are later than the bulk of 19th century majolica which interests most collectors but are generally included in collections. They represent a continuation of the spirit and feeling of Victorian era Majolica and can stand on their own as representatives of their period. At the same time the

Austrians potted vast quantities of earthenware including an endless variety of figural tobacco humidors which are quite popular among collectors.

The experienced collector can generally distinguish American and English majolica from that produced in other countries, but American and English are difficult to separate unless the pieces are marked. Since many Englishmen moved to this country, bringing their molds and glaze formulas with them, it is easy to understand why, in many instances, the craftsmanship and motifs are so similar if not identical. Wares of other countries tend to be lighter in weight and do not usually display the typical motifs, construction, brushstroke markings, and glaze colors typically found on pieces of the period (1850-1900). Many collectors limit their collections to pieces of American and English origin and it is probably safe to say that pieces from these countries are the most highly prized and collectible. The inclusion of figural pieces from the other majolica producing countries previously mentioned probably encompasses the array of pieces most avidly sought by collectors today.

PRICING

The prices listed represent a low to high range of prices for which majolica has sold in the Northeast United States. These figures were taken from shows, auctions, and dealers. However, it is possible to find many pieces at less than the listed price with some diligent searching. Many dealers not experienced in pricing and selling majolica may place the same price on a rare piece as on a more common one. Prices also tend to be higher near the east coast and drop somewhat as one travels west. The price ranges quoted here are typical "east coast" prices and an allowance has to be made when pricing in an area of the country where majolica collecting has not yet caught on, or where generally lower prices prevail.

Pieces are more often correctly priced when the dealer or collector takes into account the various desirable features a piece may possess. An attractive floral pitcher may be correctly priced at $95.00-125.00, but the same piece with the addition of a bird or a fan may be more properly priced at $125.00-150.00. The addition of a potter's mark allowing one to identify the maker may place the value even higher. However, in general, marks in themselves do not add a great deal of value for the typical collector if the piece itself does not display other virtues. More important than any mark is the level of craftsmanship, glaze colors and an appealing motif. Keep this in mind if you have the tendency to collect by mark alone and are concerned with the value of your collection. The beautifully detailed and glazed unmarked piece is usually a good investment and should be chosen over a common marked example. If the marked piece is rare and unusual such as the Etruscan cow covered butter dish (see photo in Covered Pieces section) it has excellent investment potential even though it is not too interestingly detailed or colored.

CONDITION

Most examples of 19th century Victorian majolica did not survive their one hundred years or so of existence without some small reminder of the past. This shows up in age lines (hairline cracks) at the least and huge missing chunks, missing lids, or open cracks at the worst. The mint perfect piece of majolica (showing absolutely no sign of use or age) is rare indeed. Most collectors do not limit themselves to mint condition pieces only, as to do so would severely limit the scope of their collection and many wonderful and important examples would go unrepresented. In fact, a collection assembled with condition as the prime factor would be bland indeed, consisting largely of common pieces and lacking many of those that lend depth and scope. A rare and unusual piece should be accepted in spite of repair (hopefully it was skillfully done) but common pieces should always be rejected by the serious collector if they display major repair or damage. Hairlines are hardly ever given serious consideration by the majolica collector. A good test to determine if an apparent hairline is actually a loose crack is to hold the piece to one's ear and wiggle both sides. If the crack is loose, it will have a crunching sound. If a true hairline or ageline, the piece will be silent!

Many pieces will be found in a stained condition, the result of years of use and the porous surface of this soft pottery. Although staining affects the appearance, it can usually be alleviated by a professional pottery cleaning process. One word of warning — Never attempt to use chlorine bleach to clean majolica as it may cause an eventual separation of the glaze from the body. This type of cleaning can destroy a beautiful piece.

Value is affected to some extent by condition. All values given here are for pieces in perfect condition. Small chips, age lines, and repairs do affect value somewhat, directly proportional to rarity. Defects devalue a common piece quite a bit while a skillfully done repair may not affect the value at all for an exceptionally rare piece.

BASKETS

CORSET LACED BASKET. $200.00-250.00. 11½″ l. The beautifully whimsical detail of corset lacing repeated around this basket sets it apart.

BIRD IN FLIGHT EGG CUP BASKET. $200.00-250.00. 9½″ l. Six circular openings in the top are filled with little mottled egg cups, each with a lavender lining. One cup is missing here.

CABBAGE LEAF AND DAISY BASKET. $200.00-250.00. 12½" l. This basket has everything! Little yellow feet, and wonderful luggage strap handles.

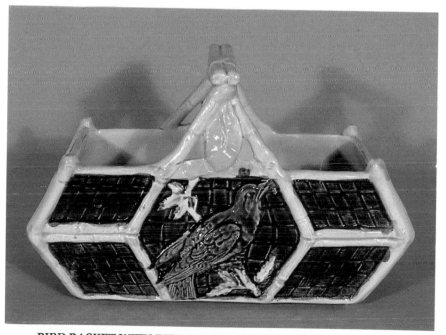

BIRD BASKET WITH RIBBON TIED HANDLE. $150.00-200.00. 10" l.

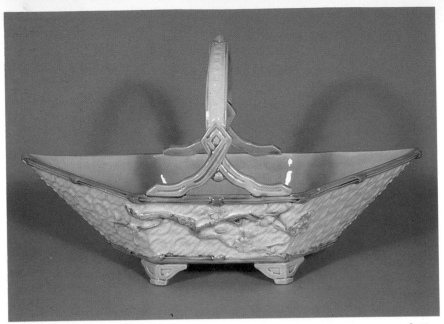

ORNATE HANDLED FOOTED FLORAL BASKET. $225.00-250.00. 15¼″ l. Exceptionally large with interesting details on the handle and feet.

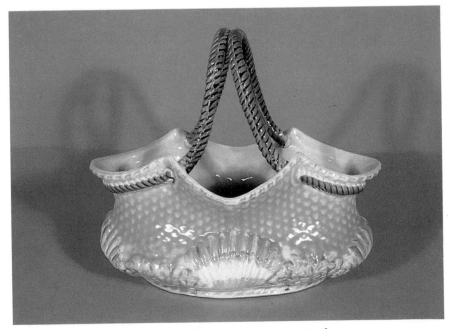

SHELL BASKET. $150.00-200.00. 8½″ l.

BIRD'S NEST BASKET. $125.00-175.00. 9½" l.

BANKS AND THORLEY BAMBOO AND BASKETWEAVE BASKET. $95.00-145.00 Part of the large series produced by this English company located in Hanley.

BASKETWEAVE BASKET WITH RIBBON TIED HANDLE. $125.00-175.00. 10" l.

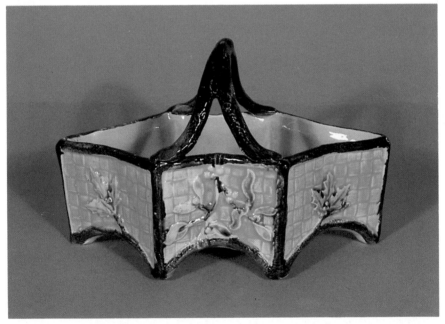

SIX SIDED FLORAL BASKET. $125.00-150.00 6" l. approx.

BOWLS AND SERVING DISHES

ETRUSCAN OAK FRUIT TRAY. $175.00-240.00. 12″ l. This monumental bowl was produced by Griffin, Smith and Hill, Phoenixville, Pennsylvania and bears the circular Etruscan Majolica mark. Also with a white background.

TURQUOISE SCALLOPED TOP FLORAL BOWL. $150.00-195.00. 9″ d. 4″ h.

CHESTNUT LEAF ON FOLDED NAPKIN BOWL. $125.00-165.00. 9" d. 2¾" h. This bowl was produced from a George Jones mold but it is unsigned. Quite possibly a copy by one of Jones' contempories.

ETRUSCAN SHELL SALAD BOWL. $195.00-250.00. 8¼" d. This style with seashells around the footed base is much more rare than the unfooted bowl. Circular Etruscan Majolica mark.

ETRUSCAN DAISY SAUCE DISH. $115.00-135.00. 8¼" l. This came in two sizes and matches the Daisy Salad Comport.

SHORTER & BOULTON BIRD AND FAN SAUCE DISHES. $35.00-55.00. 5" d.
Shorter and Boulton, Stoke, England, registered this design on March 17, 1881.
They all bear the English Registry mark. These are a good example of dif-
ference in quality of glaze. While the bowl on the left has perfectly acceptably
coloring, the one on the right is much more intense and desirable.

WARDLE BIRD AND FAN FOOTED VEGETABLE BOWL. $95.00-125.00. 10" l.
Manufactured by Wardle & Co., Hanley, England. One of a large series of
pieces produced by this company, they all bear the English Registry mark.

ETRUSCAN SHELL AND SEAWEED BOWLS. $165.00-185.00. 8½″ d. $145.00-185.00. 5″ d. The bowl on the left is the waste bowl to the shell and seaweed teaset.

PICKET FENCE BOWL. $110.00-135.00 9″ d. The interior has an unusual turquoise, brown, and white mottling instead of the more traditional lavender or turquoise.

TWIG HANDLED FOOTED BOWL. $85.00-125.00. 9". This was also made with serpent handles and without handles. The color of the flowers will vary.

WARDLE SUNFLOWER BOWL. $110.00-145.00. 10½" l. This design was registered to Wardle & Co., Hanley, England, on July 19, 1882, patent #383641. Also in a platter.

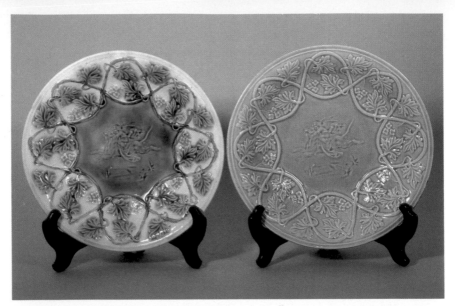

ETRUSCAN CLASSICAL SERIES BOWLS. R. to L. $75.00-95.00. $110.00-145.00. 9¾" d. These are part of the large classical series produced by Griffin, Smith, and Hill depicting mythological scenes. Pieces of this series occur most often in the all over sepia coloring shown on the bowl at right. The colorful glaze treatment on the left is more scarce.

HOLDCROFT TWIG FOOTED BOWL. $225.00-275.00. 10½" l. Marked with the monogram JH in a circle. See mark No. 5.

HOLDCROFT POND LILY BOWL. $95.00-125.00. 11″ d. Impressed J. Holdcroft.
See mark No. 4.

DUCK WASTE BOWL. $35.00-55.00. 5½″ d. Part of the teaset. Look for a sugar
bowl and cream pitcher among others.

COMPOTES AND CAKESTANDS

ETRUSCAN DAISY SALAD COMPORT. $110.00-145.00. 9″ d. 5″ h. These were made with a white background and a cobalt background.

GRAPE LEAF COMPOTE. $110.00-135.00. 8½″ d. 4½″ h. This is a copy of a Wedgwood pattern.

SHELL AND SEAWEED LOW CAKESTAND. $95.00-125.00. 8½" d. 2¼" h. Part of a large series of pieces which included a cake plate, cup and saucer, bowl, and a high cakestand among others.

NEW ENGLAND ASTOR CAKE STAND. $65.00-95.00. 9" d. 2" h. Many pieces were produced in this pattern which is attributed to James Scollay Taft of the Hampshire Pottery, Keene, N.H. Look for a large vegetable bowl, platter, plates, teapot, mug, butter pats, teaset, spooner, high cake stand and a spice tray with handle.

WORCESTER DOLPHIN COMPOTE. $200.00-295.00. 9″ d. 7″ h. Possibly the piece copied by Griffin, Smith and Hill when they produced their L2 dolphin comport, this is almost identical except for the base. The Worcester mark is impressed underneath inside the pedestal. see mark No. 8.

SHELL COMPOTE. $75.00-110.00. 9″ d. 6″ h. This large handsome salad bowl is attributed to Morley. They were produced in yellow and turquoise.

PINEAPPLE COMPOTE. $115.00-145.00. 9″ d. 4¾″ h. One of the major majolica motifs, a large variety of ware was produced in the pineapple pattern.

WILD ROSE AND ROPE COMPOTE. $125.00-150.00. 9¾″ d. 6″ h. Also in a turquoise background.

FIELDING SNAIL SHELL HIGH CAKE STAND. $120.00-160.00. 9½″ d. 5¼″ h. English Registry mark and FIELDING impressed see mark No. 6. Part of a series of fishnet covered pieces displaying a variety of seashells. Includes pitchers, teapot, sugar and cream pitcher, and a low cakestand.

COBALT BELLFLOWER COMPOTE. $120.00-150.00. 9½″ d. 5″ h. Also in a plate.

LEAF ON PLATE LOW CAKESTAND. $110.00-145.00. 9″ d.

BROWN, WESTHEAD, MOORE & CO. COMPOTE. $200.00-250.00. 8½" d. 7" h.
The name is impressed on the underside of one of the twig feet. Marked
English pieces such as this are rare and desirable. Rare mark.

PIECES WITH COVERS: SARDINE BOXES, BUTTER DISHES, CHEESE KEEPERS

WILD ROSE BUTTER DISH WITH ROPE TRIM. $110.00-150.00. 6½" d. This pattern was produced in a variety of pieces including platters, teasets, plates, and compotes. The background colors vary and include cobalt, blue-grey and turquoise.

COBALT AND SEAWEED SARDINE BOX. $200.00-250.00. 7½" l. Attached underplate.

GEORGE JONES SARDINE BOX. $275.00-325.00. 8½" l. 7¾" w. Both the box and the separate underplate are signed. These pieces display all the beauty of color and quality of workmanship one expects from a George Jones piece. Also in a turquoise background. The box and the underplate will be found both with a variety of marks and unmarked. See marks No. 1, 2, and 3.

RASPBERRY BUTTER DISH. $95.00-125.00. 7" d. Rustic tree bark background with a mottled green and brown glaze.

COW FINIAL CHEESE KEEPER. $750.00-1000.00. 11½" h. 12¾" d. This is truly a monumental piece. Unsigned, but the workmanship and coloring allow an attribution to the pottery of George Jones, Stoke on Trent.

ETRUSCAN COW BUTTER DISH. $450.00-550.00. 7¾″ d. This is one of the rarest Etruscan pieces. Also in yellow and green mottling.

GEORGE JONES DUCK FINIAL SARDINE BOX. $300.00-395.00. 5¾″ l. This large beaked fellow has had some restoration to his head and the original beak was probably much smaller. Unusual to find a sardine box with other than a fish finial. Rare.

AVALON "SUNNY BANK" PUSH-UP TOBACCO HUMIDOR. $110.00-125.00. 9″ h. "Sunny Bank" is the name of the tobacco produced by Spaulding & Merrick in Chicago. A nice example of majolica produced as advertising by the Chesapeake Pottery Company. Printed Avalon Faience mark.

HOLLY CHEESE KEEPER. $400.00-600.00. 10½″ h. 10½″ d.

SWAN FINIAL SARDINE BOX WITH DOLPHIN FEET. $225.00-275.00. 5¾″ l. A beautiful swan preening his feathers and gliding through pond lily leaves. The four dolphin feet and the cobalt ground add to an already outstanding piece. An example of excellence in design.

SHELL, SEAWEED, AND WAVES BUTTER DISH. $125.00-150.00. 7" d.

GEORGE JONES DOGWOOD AND WOVEN FENCE CHEESE KEEPER. $650.00-850.00. 10½" h. 11½" d. Impressed with the English Registry mark and the JG monogram. See mark No. 3. Also in a teaset with tray, a small pitcher and a smaller version of this keeper without the fence. The impressive skills of one of England's finest craftsmen is presented in full form here! Superb.

ETRUSCAN SHELL CIGAR BOX. $450.00-550.00. One of the rarest pieces in Griffin, Smith and Hill's shell and seaweed series.

SUNFLOWER WITH FLY BUTTER DISH. $110.00-135.00. 6¾" d.

CONCH SHELL AND BASKETWEAVER SARDINE BOX. $145.00-175.00. 8½" L.
A nice design employing a shell finial instead of the more typical fish. The
underplate is attached.

COBALT AND FLORAL BUTTER DISH. $150.00-195.00. 7½" d. The cobalt blue adds extra value.

"UNDER THE SEA" SCENE SARDINE BOX. $225.00-300.00. 6½" d. Unusual form around the base.

COBALT AND LEAFY GARLAND SARDINE BOX. $200.00-250.00. 9½" l. Nice workmanship and color. Attached underplate.

BASKET OF FISH SARDINE BOX. $250.00-300.00. 8½" l. Unusual open handles on the attached underplate. A prize example, probably George Jones.

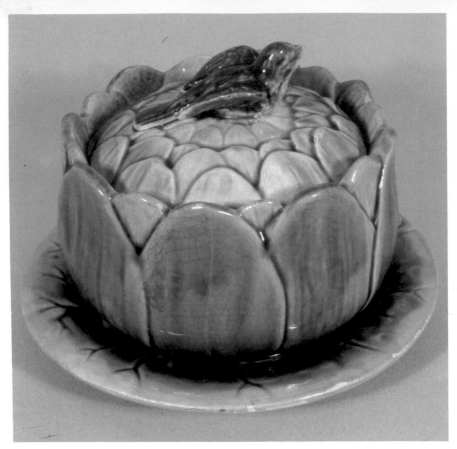

BIRD ATOP ARTICHOKE COVERED BOWL. $175.00-200.00. 7¼″ d.

POND LILY AND BAMBOO SARDINE BOX. $250.00-300.00. 9″ l. Impressed V.P.C. with two swords forming a triangle.

MINTON SARDINE BOX. $450.00-550.00. 9″ l. Impressed Minton. Attached underplate. Minton pieces are among the finest.

POINTED LEAVES SARDINE BOX. $225.00-300.00. 9″ d. Attached underplate.

BANKS AND THORLEY BASKETWEAVE AND BAMBOO COVERED BUTTER DISH. $150.00-195.00. 8″ d.

ETRUSCAN BAMBOO COVERED BUTTER DISH. $225.00-250.00. 6½" d.

YELLOW BASKETWEAVE SARDINE BOX. $125.00-165.00. 5½" l.

CHEESE WEDGE WITH WHEAT HANDLE. $125.00-145.00. 5¾″ h. 9¾″ l.

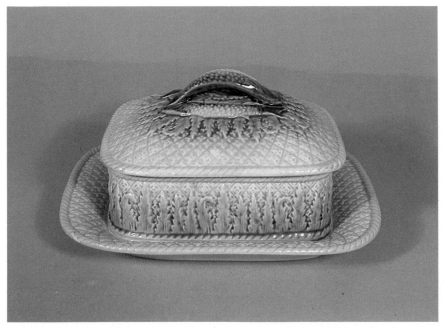

PINEAPPLE SARDINE BOX. $150.00-195.00. 9½″ l. Attached underplate.

FIGURAL PIECES

PELICAN PITCHER. $200.00-250.00. 9″ h. Unusual handle on a very desirable figural piece.

WING HANDLED DUCK BEAK-POURING PITCHER. $95.00-125.00. 11″ h. Marked "Made in Portugal". 20th century. A type of brightly colored faience pottery resembling majolica and included in collections of figural pieces.

TOBACCO HUMIDORS. L. to R. BULLDOG WITH MUG OF BEER HUMIDOR. $125.00-145.00. 7¾″ h. **"ALICE" BULLDOG HUMIDOR. $65.00-95.00.** 4″ h. Hat impressed "Alice". **FROG STRUMMING A MANDOLIN HUMIDOR. $125.00-145.00.** 6¾″ h.

PIG WAITER MOUTH POURING PITCHER. $175.00-195.00. 10¾". One of a number of interesting French pieces by a producer who marked his wares Frie Onnang, and sometimes included crown and shield.

PARROTT PITCHER. $195.00-245.00 11¼" h. This stately bird is remarkable for his size and the good detail and coloring of his feathers. Made in a variety of sizes, this was probably the largest. Many smaller examples do not display the high relief of the feathers and good coloring of this specimen.

PAIR OF MOUTH-POURING PUG PITCHERS. R. to L. $200.00-250.00. 10½" h. $150.00-200.00. 7½" h. These wonderful looking fellows have hand-carved-teeth and the larger of the two has rake-like scratches in his clay to simulate fur. Most unusual and thought to be American.

MORLEY OWL PITCHER. $145.00-195.00. 8¼" h. Marked MORLEY & CO. MAJOLLICA, WELLSVILLE, O. The glazing is done in typical majolica style on white ironstone instead of the usual earthenware. These pieces are particularly desirable because they are figural, marked, and American.

42

MORLEY FISH BOUQUET HOLDER.
$95.00-125.00. 6¾" h. Marked
GEORGE MORLEY'S MAJOLICA.
EAST LIVERPOOL, O. Morley also
made a large fish but the detailing
and workmanship is not as good as
the small "bouquet holder".

FRENCH FAIENCE BEAK-POURING
ROOSTER PITCHER. $85.00-125.00.
12" h. This is not a typical majolica
glaze.

FRENCH FAIENCE BEAK-POURING
PAROTT PITCHER. $75.00-95.00. 11"
h.

BISON HEAD COVERED JAR.
$95.00-120.00. 5" h. Incised in
freehand script, "Austria".

MUGS

PANSY SHAVING MUG. $110.00-
145.00. 3½″ h. Quite rare, the
lavender interior has a divider with a
section for the shaving lather.
Straight line impressed mark, probably Fielding.

ETRUSCAN ACORN MUG. $110.00-
145.00. 3½″ h.

ETRUSCAN FOOTED LILY MUG.
$95.00-135.00. 4″ h. These are never
signed.

HOLDCROFT LILY MUG. $65.00-
95.00. 3½″ h. Impressed J. Holdcroft.

PICKET FENCE AND FLORAL MUG.
$45.00-65.00. 3¾″.

COBALT WITH TRAILING IVY
MUG. $75.00-65.00. 4″ h.

R. to L. All 3½" h. COBALT MUG WITH SUNFLOWER. $45.00-65.00. CLIFTON
DECOR MUG. $55.00-75.00. Printed "Clifton Decor" mark. See mark No. 11.
ETRUSCAN PINEAPPLE MUG. $75.00-95.00. Marked only with the decorators
black stenciled number, these mugs are always attributed to Griffin, Smith,
and Hill but are never marked with the GSH monogram.

FROG AND FERN ON BAMBOO MUG. $110.00-150.00. 4½" h. Two figural
frogs surprise the unwary drinker when he nears the bottom!

PITCHERS

WARDLE FERN AND BAMBOO PITCHER. $110.00-150.00. 7½" h. Part of the large fern and bamboo series produced by this English company. English Registry mark.

BANKS AND THORLEY BASKETWEAVE AND BAMBOO PITCHER. $75.00-115.00. 7½" h.

FLORAL PITCHER. $95.00-125.00. 7" h.

BIRD AND POND LILY PITCHER. $110.00-145.00. 8" h.

STORK IN A MARSH WITH OVERHEAD FISH. $150.00-175.00. 9". This wonderful pitcher has such an interesting motif with a bamboo base and a large stork standing in the marsh complete with cattails. What appears to be a bird flying overhead, upon closer inspection, is actually a fish. I have no explanation other than a flight of fancy on the part of the artist.

BLACKBERRY PITCHER. $75.00-110.00. 7½" approx.

TREE TRUNK AND FLORAL PITCHER. $75.00-110.00. 7" h. This closely copies a Wedgwood design.

ETRUSCAN RUSTIC PITCHER. $135.00-165.00. 8¼" h. Griffin, Smith, and Hill potted these in 5 sizes.

BEVINGTON SWAN ON PITCHER. $165.00-195.00. 8½″ h. This design was registered to the firm of J. Bevington, Hanley, England on November 21, 1881, patent #373575. Remarkable because of its unusual form, the swan pours through its tail feathers with the neck forming the handle. English Registry mark.

FLORAL TURQUOISE BANDED PITCHER. $85.00-125.00. 8¼″ h.

WATER LILY AND DRAGONFLY PITCHER. $95.00-135.00. 7½″ h. A lily bud atop the handle and the dragonfly make this an unusual piece.

TURQUOISE AND BASKETWEAVE THREE LEAF PITCHER. $95.00-135.00. 8″ h. This came in graduated sizes, including a small syrup pitcher with a pewter lid.

WEDGEWOOD BIRD AND FAN
PITCHER. $450.00-550.00. 10" h.
Wedgwood's beautiful color and
detail combined with the enormous
size make this an outstanding piece.
Probably made for display only,
when full, it is too heavy to handle.
Impressed Wedgwood.

LITTLE GIRL AND DOG PITCHER.
$85.00-110.00. 8" h. Highly unusual in
that it features a little girl. Designers
of this period followed an unwritten
rule and generally did not include
people in their designs.

REINDEER PITCHER. $75.00-110.00.
7½".

BIRDS NEST PITCHER. $95.00-125.00.
9¼". This is typical of the work of an
unknown potter (probably American)
who made a variety of pieces with
these "tree knurls" protruding
around the base.

SYRUP PITCHERS. $95.00-120.00 each. 4¾″ to 6″ h. Many of the larger pitchers were also made in these diminuitive sizes with pewter lids.

FIGURAL CREAM PITCHERS. $65.00-95.00. 4½″ approx. This spaniel and owl are collectible as figurals, as cream pitchers, and as majolica.

FISH ON WAVES PITCHER. $150.00-195.00. 8¼". Beautiful coloring and lusterous glaze. There is another pitcher with the identical form but a slightly different handle and one similar to this, but with a different top and bearing the English Registry mark. This is unmarked. A splendid example of a fish pitcher.

HOLDCROFT PEWTER TOP LILY PITCHER. $125.00-150.00. 4¾" h. Impressed J. Holdcroft.

BUTTERFLY AND FLORAL CREAM PITCHER. $45.00-65.00. 3½" h.

MAPLE LEAF PEWTER TOP SYRUP PITCHER. $120.00-150.00. 7" h.

GEORGE JONES MONKEY HAN-
DLED PITCHER. $250.00-350.00. 7" h.
English Registry mark. Also in a
teaset on tray.

PEWTER TOPPED PINEAPPLE
SYRUP PITCHER. $95.00-125.00. 5¼".

BIRD AND IRIS FOOTED CREAM PITCHER. $65.00-85.00. 4" h. Compare this
to the Etruscan Bird and Iris pattern — nearly identical except this example is
footed.

FAN AND SCROLL WITH INSECT PITCHERS. R. to L. $110.00-145.00. $85.00-110. 5½" h. 4½" h. English Registry mark. This interesting pattern always combines a fan with a small insect and a scroll bearing an impressed clipper ship. Other pieces in this pattern with the impressed maker's mark allow an attribution to S. Fielding & Co., Stoke, England.

RUSTIC BLACKBERRY PITCHER WITH TREE KNURL BASE. $65.00-95.00. 5½" h.

STORK IN MARSH WITH EEL HANDLE PITCHER. $165.00-195.00. 9½" h. This is a splendid example of a bird pitcher with colorful cattails, a smaller bird and a figural handle which could be an eel.

COPELAND EGYPTIAN LOTUS PITCHERS. $325.00-375.00. 8¼" h. $275.00-325.00. 6½" h. Clearly a masterpiece of design and workmanship these pitchers rank among the highest achievements for English potters of the period. Impressed COPELAND along with the English Registry mark, the design was registered on July 2, 1877, patent #311523. The larger is impressed 6.Gill and the smaller is impressed 3.Gill above the registry mark.

GEORGE JONES DOGWOOD PITCHER AND CHEESE KEEPER LID. R. to L. $95.00-145.00. 5½" h. $65.00-95.00 lid only. 8" d. The pitcher design was registered to George Jones, Stoke, England, on February 25, 1873, patent #270700. It has the English registry mark only and no George Jones signature. The lid to the small cheese keeper is in the same pattern. Jones also produced a tea service and tray with the dogwood design. Refer to the "Covered Pieces" section to view this pattern in all its magnificence as a large cheese keeper.

WILD ROSE ON TREE BARK PITCHER. $110.00-145.00. 9½" h. A beautiful example of this fairly common pattern. In addition to the turquoise pictured here, it came in additional background colors of white and brown. This piece is particularly large.

ETRUSCAN WILD ROSE PITCHER. $135.00-165.00. 8" h. The wild rose pitcher with its butterfly lip was produced in a variety of sizes, the smallest being a tiny cream pitcher.

PEWTER TOPPED CORN PITCHER. $175.00-195.00. 9½" h. The English registry mark, pewter top, rich color of the glazes, gracefullness of form, and the stately size combine to make this a beautiful example of England's rendition of the corn pattern. Many corn pattern pieces were also produced in America.

ROBIN ON BRANCH PITCHER. $75.00-95.00. 7½" h. The same unknown potter also produced a very similar design but with a different style of bird. Coloration varies.

BARK SQUARES WITH KNURLED BASE PITCHER. $85.00-125.00. 7½" h. Also made in a teaset.

MERMAID PITCHER. $250.00-350.00. 9½" h. approx. Unusual figural handle and high quality relief work and glazing. Attributed to J. Holdcroft, Longton, England.

ETRUSCAN SHELL AND SEAWEED PITCHERS. R. to L. $125.00-155.00. 3½" h. $200.00-285.00. 5¾" h. $160.00-195.00. 4¾" h. $200.00-285.00. 6¾" h. Considered to be one of the most beautiful patterns ever made by Griffin, Smith and Hill, these pieces are avidly sought by most collectors. Shell patterns and marine themes were one of the most popular majolica motifs. Look for other shell motifs produced by Wedgwood, Fielding, and James Carr of the New York City Pottery Co., among others.

PINEAPPLE PITCHER. $135.00-
165.00. 8″ h.

SHARKSKIN AND FLORAL BOW
PITCHER. $110.00-145.00. 8¼″ h.

BLACKBERRY AND PICKET FENCE
PITCHER. $45.00-65.00. 7″ h.

BASKETWEAVE AND FENCE
FLORAL PITCHER. $45.00-65.00. 6″ h.

SQUARE TOPPED FLORAL
PITCHER. $45.00-65.00. 6″ h.

BIRD AND BASKETWEAVE
PITCHER. $95.00-135.00. 8½″ h.

ETRUSCAN SUNFLOWER PITCHER.
$150.00-195.00. 6½″ h. The sunflower
pitcher was made in a variety of sizes
with three background colors. The
cobalt is pictured here. They also
came in white and pink.

BLACKBERRY PITCHER. $145.00-
195.00. 8″ h. This is the king of the
blackberry pieces with its good
workmanship, vibrant coloring, and
large size.

WAVY BACKGROUND FLORAL
PITCHER. $85.00-125.00. 8″ h.
Unusual for the curved background
and the grey imbossed handle.

LEAF SPOUT FLORAL AND BARK
PITCHER. $95.00-135.00. 7″ h. Careful
workmanship and lusterous glazes
combine with an unusual leaf
treatment.

OAK BARREL AND AVOCADO
PITCHER. $115.00-145.00. 5½″ h. Un-
marked but possibly George Jones.
Heavy green and brown mottled
base.

LEAF SPOUT AND ROSE AND
BASKETWEAVE PITCHER. $125.00-
165.00. 9¼″ h. The immense size
distinguishes this one. Made in
various smaller sizes, this is probably
the largest.

GEORGE JONES IRIS AND LILY PITCHER. $250.00-350.00. 6¾″ h. Perfectly exquisite, it is not difficult to see why George Jones majolica is considered among the best. GJ monogram is in a circle.

WICKER SYRUP PITCHER (missing pewter lid). $115.00-145.00 if lid present. 6¼″ h. Attributed to George Jones. Lavender base.

BLACKBERRY FENCE PITCHER. $45.00-55.00. 7¼″ h.

OWL AND FAN TRIANGULAR PITCHER. $120.00-165.00. 7½″ h. Beautiful in every aspect with a fan spout, bamboo handle, and bamboo leaves on the back. These were made in a variety of sizes. There is at least one size larger. Also with a grey background.

**ALL TAN-HAWTHORNE PITCHER.
$95.00-125.00.** 5¼" h. These are
always unsigned but are considered
to be Etruscan. They also occur in
all-over green and all-over cobalt.
The reason for the unconventional
decoration and the unsigned base re-
mains a mystery. They could have
been a special "budget" order for
some retail outlet, an experimenta-
tion with a less costly method of
operation by Griffin, Smith, and Hill
themselves, or pieces given free of
charge to the pottery workers for
their own use.

**MORLEY SYRUP PITCHER. $145.00-
165.00.** 8¼" h. Also on white
ironstone as are the Morley owl and
fish bouquet holder. The base is
marked MORLEY & CO.
WELLSVILLE, O.

ETRUSCAN ALBINO SHELL PITCHER. $110.00-145.00. 5¾" h. The base bears
the circular Etruscan Majolica mark.

BENT TREE TRUNK PITCHER.
$95.00-115.00. 7" h.

BOW AND FLORAL SYRUP
PITCHER. $125.00-145.00. 8¼" h.

BENNETTS SUNFLOWER SYRUP
PITCHER. $125.00-145.00. 7¾" h.
Marked BENNETT'S JAN. 28, 1873,
PATENT. This is the year the design
was registered with the patent office
and not necessarily the year of
manufacture.

ETRUSCAN SUNFLOWER SYRUP
PITCHER. $150.00-195.00. 8" h. These
lovely pieces were produced with
cobalt background as shown here and
also with a white and a pink ground.

ETRUSCAN BAMBOO SYRUP
PITCHER. $175.00-275.00. 8″ h. These
have recently gone at wildly
divergent prices, both lower and
higher than those listed here.

ADAMS AND BROMLEY LILY
PITCHER. $125.00-165.00. 8″ h. This
design was registered to Adams and
Bromley of Hanley, England, on
August 21, 1882, patent #385129.
English registry mark.

BAMBOO AND BOW PEWTER TOP
PITCHER. $120.00-150.00. 6″ h.

RUNNING ELEPHANT PITCHER.
$95.00-125.00. 7½″ h.

ETRUSCAN CORAL SYRUP PITCHER. $150.00-200.00. 6¼″ h. The small size sets this apart from other Etruscan syrup pitchers.

ENGLISH COTTAGE PITCHER. $200.00-250.00. 7″ h. Quite unusual and well done.

FERN ON BARK PEWTER TOP PITCHER. $120.00-145.00. 7″ h.

STORK WITH FISH IN MOUTH PITCHER. $200.00-250.00. 8¼″ h. A very desirable piece with beautiful high relief and very careful decoration. The artistry of design is quite evident here. The pattern was also produced by George Jones.

BANKS AND THORLEY PEWTER TOP SYRUP PITCHER. $125.00-150.00. 7½" h. English registry mark.

PEAS IN POD PEWTER TOP PITCHER. $110.00-145.00. 5½" h. Also in a larger version without the pewter top.

ROBIN ON A BRANCH PEWTER TOP PITCHER. $110.00-145.00. 4½" h. Remarkable for its tiny size. Also in a larger version without the pewter top.

CLIFTON DECOR FRUIT PATTERN PITCHER. $110.00-145.00. 6½" h. Clifton decor mark. See mark No. 11.

SAMUEL LEAR SUNFLOWER AND CLASSICAL URN CREAM PITCHER. $45.00-65.00. 3½" h. Part of a large series including platters, plates, cakestands, and a mustache cup and saucer. English registry mark.

ETRUSCAN CORN CREAM PITCHER. $75.00-95.00. 4" h. These can be marked with the catalog number only, E5, or with the decorator's black stenciled identification number only.

COBALT PEWTER TOPPED PITCHER. $110.00-135.00. 4½" h.

JRL FISH PITCHER. $125.00-150.00. 7" h. Impressed JRL on the footrim. Possibly J. Roth, London, who registered designs c. 1882.

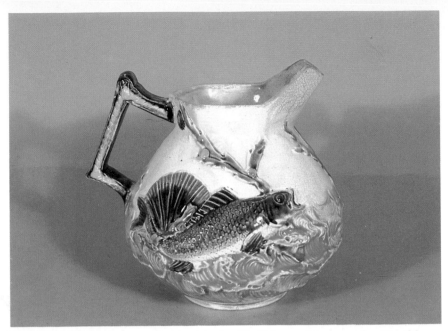

FISH PITCHER. $125.00-150.00. 7½" h. English registry mark. Possibly Shorter & Boulton.

WARDLE BIRD AND FAN PITCHER. $150.00-185.00. 7¼" h. Also in a larger size and cream pitcher size. English registry mark.

DRAGON HANDLED FLORAL PITCHER. $175.00-225.00. 8¼" h. Unusual winged dragon figural handle. Also in a larger size with a yellow background.

ETRUSCAN FERN PITCHER. $175.00-225.00. 8¼" h. Potted in a variety of sizes.

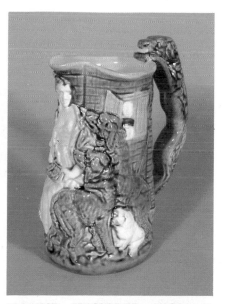

FAN, BUTTERFLY AND CRICKET PITCHER. $125.00-165.00. 8¾" h.

HOUND HANDLED WOMAN FEEDING DOGS PITCHER. $195.00-210.00. 6" h. Very rare hound handle. Also unusual for majolica of this period to portray a woman.

GREEN LEAF AND FLORAL PITCHER. $125.00-145.00. 7″ h. Probably Holdcroft.

FIELDING SHELL AND FISHNET PITCHER. $175.00-225.00. 7″ h. Also in a teapot, cream pitcher, lidded sugar bowl, and a waste bowl. English registry mark.

ARRAY OF CREAM PITCHERS AND A SPOONER. R. to L. OWL AND FAN SPOONER. $75.00-95.00. 4½″ h. FIGURAL FISH CREAM PITCHER. $75.00-95.00. 3¼″ h. FISH HANDLED ANCHOR CREAM PITCHER. $45.00-65.00. 4½″ h.

COBALT AND FLORAL PITCHER. $75.00-95.00. 5½″ h.

PLATES, PLATTERS, BREAD TRAYS, FANS, OYSTER PLATES AND BUTTER PATS

FLYING CRANE AND WATER LILY PLATTER. $75.00-110.00. 10½" d. Produced in a variety of pieces. Includes vases, cups and saucers, luncheon plates, fruit dishes, and a small bowl and milk pitcher.

FIELDING FAN PLATE. $50.00-75.00. 8¾" d. Impressed FIELDING. These were produced both signed and unsigned.

TWO PARROTS ON A BRANCH PLATE. $45.00-75.00. 8½" d.

FAN AND DRAGONFLY PLATTER. $95.00-125.00. 10½″ l.

BAMBOO AND BOW PLATTER. $125.00-175.00. 13" l.

FIELDING FAN ICE CREAM TRAY. $200.00-250.00. 14½" l. Impressed English registry mark and FIELDING.

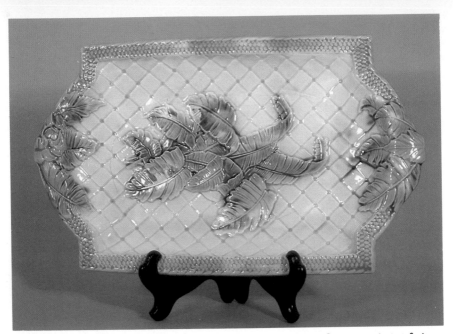

BANANA LEAVES PLATTER. $110.00-150.00. 14″ l. Potted in a variety of sizes and colors.

DIAMOND SHAPED FLORAL PLATTER. $75.00.-110.00. 12″ l.

SUNFLOWER PLATTER. $95.00-125.00. 12½" l. English registry mark. Attributed to Wardle & Co., Hanley.

WEDGWOOD FRUIT PLATTER AND 12 PLATES. $350.00-550.00 the set. Platter 15½" l. Plates 7" d.

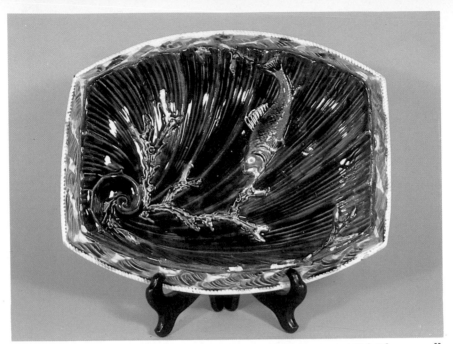

FISH AND CORAL WITH WAVES PLATTER. $110.00-145.00. 13″ l. The overall shape and the waves on the outer edge are a direct copy of a Wedgwood piece.

CORN BREAD TRAY. $110.00-145.00. 12″ l.

DRAGONFLY ON LEAF PLATTER. $75.00-95.00. 11″ l.

LEAVES AND FERN PLATTER. $75.00-110.00. 12″ l.

SCALLOPED EDGE DOG AND DOGHOUSE PLATTER. $85.00-110.00 11″ l.

ETRUSCAN CLASSICAL SERIES PLATE. $75.00-95.00. 9″ h. Marked with the GSH monogram. See mark No. 10.

STRAWBERRIES AND LEAVES PLATE. $55.00-75.00. 8¾″ d.

FLORAL AND THREE LEAF PLATE. $45.00-55.00. 9″ d.

MOTTLED CENTER PLATES. R. to L. Etruscan Bamboo plate. $65.00-100.00. 8″ d. Cobalt border and floral plate. $65.00-95.00. 9½″ d. This may be an underplate missing the lid. Etruscan Rose plate. $55.00-75.00. 7″ d. Etruscan underplate to the Lily cheese keeper. $75.00-95.00. 11½″ d. Also produced as a bread tray. In that form it lacks the ridge to hold the top in place which is present on this piece.

ETRUSCAN MAPLE LEAVES PLATE. $75.00-110.00. 9″ d. Pictured here in the pink and white backgrounds, it was probably also produced in blue.

MORLEY NAPKIN PLATE. $75.00-110.00. 8″ h. Marked MORLEY & CO. MAJOLLICA, WELLSVILLE, O. White ironstone instead of the earthenware body.

ETRUSCAN LEAF ON PLATE. $45.00-65.00. 7¾″ d. Also in an 8¾″ d.

ETRUSCAN GRAPE FRUIT DISH. $85.00-110.00. 6½″ d. This is the individual fruit dish that accompanies the oval grape fruit tray. This was done with background colors of white, as shown, pink and lavender, as was the grape fruit tray.

SHELL AND CORAL CAKE PLATE. $95.00-150.00. 11″ d.

ETRUSCAN SHELL CAKE PLATTER. $200.00-250.00. 13½" l.

WARDLE'S BAMBOO AND FERN BREAD TRAY. $110.00-145.00. 13" l.

FERN AND BASKETWEAVE EDGE PLATTER. $95.00-125.00. 11¼" l.

"WASTE NOT-WANT NOT" BUTTERFLY BREAD TRAY. $125.00-150.00. 13½" l.

R. to L. All approx. 3" d. COBALT FLORAL BUTTER PAT. $16.00-25.00. FAN
AND SWALLOW BUTTER PAT. $20.00-30.00. SHELL AND SEAWEED BUT-
TER PAT. $16.00-25.00. This is a copy of the Wedgwood version.

R. to L. MORNING GLORY ON NAPKIN BUTTER PAT. $10.00-18.00. All ap-
prox. 3" d. Probably German. POINTED LEAF SHAPED BUTTER PAT. $15.00-
18.00. BEGONIA LEAF ON BASKETWEAVE BUTTER PAT. $15.00-22.00.

R. to L. ETRUSCAN POND LILY BUTTER PAT. $18.00-24.00. All approx. 3" d.
ETRUSCAN PANSY BUTTER PAT. $25.00-30.00. ETRUSCAN SMILAX BUT-
TER PAT. $35.00-55.00. The smilax pattern is rare.

WEDGWOOD BOAT PLATTER. $250.00-350.00. 14″ l. approx. Modeled to resemble a boat in water with seaweed falling in over the side as if one were looking down from overhead.

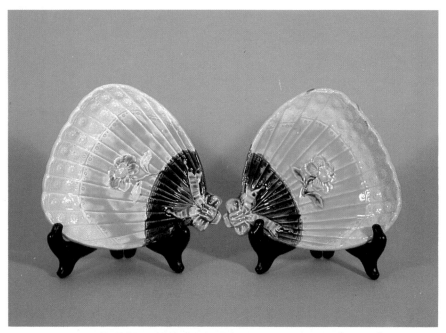

FAN AND BOW DESSERT DISHES. $55.00-75.00 each. 6½″ l.

GEORGE JONES OYSTER PLATES. $75.00-145.00. 8¾" d. Impressed with the
George Jones monogram.

WATER LILY PLATTER AND DESSERT DISHES. $225.00-295.00. 13½" l. plat-
ter. 5¼" x 4¼" dessert dish.

BEGONIA ON BARK PLATTER. $95.00-125.00. 12¼″ l. Look for this platter also in a banana leaf pattern.

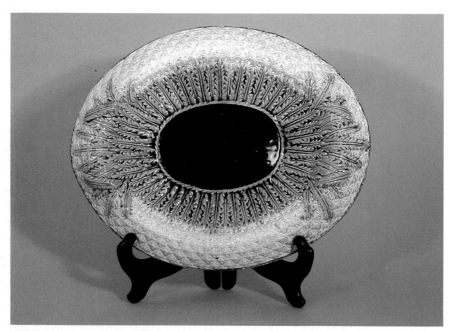

PINEAPPLE BREAD TRAY. $110.00-145.00. 13″ l. Probably Wardle & Co., Hanley, England.

ETRUSCAN SHELL AND SEAWEED PLATE. $135.00-150.00. 9″ d. The 9″ version of this Etruscan plate is much more rare than the 7″ ($85.00-110.00), or the 8″ ($95.00-115.00) sizes.

PARROT, BUTTERFLY AND BAMBOO PLATE. $50.00-75.00. 9″ d. This fellow was registered in England in 1884, and bears the impressed registry mark Rd No. 3119.

ETRUSCAN STRAWBERRY PLATE. $75.00-110.00. 9″ d. This was also produced with a white background. The blue is uncommon.

PINEAPPLE PLATE. $65.00-85.00. 9¼″ d.

STRAWBERRY AND BOW PLATTER. $165.00-195.00. 13½″ l. Also plates and teapots.

BANANA LEAVES AND BOWS PLATTER. $110.00-150.00. 14½″ l.

WEDGWOOD BASKETWEAVE
BORDER PLATE. $65.00-95.00. 9″ d.
Impressed Wedgwood.

WILD ROSE PLATE. $45.00-55.00.
8¾″ d. Also came in a platter.

HOLDCROFT FISH PLATE. $65.00-
85.00. 8½″ d. Impressed J. Holdcroft.

WEDGWOOD RETICULATED
BORDER PLATE. $75.00-95.00. 8¾″ d.

WEDGWOOD SHELL PLATE. $45.00-55.00. 8½″ d.

OVERLAPPING BEGONIA LEAVES PLATE. $35.00-45.00. 8¾″ d.

WEDGWOOD OCTAGONAL EDGE PLATE. $95.00-145.00. 9″ d.

SEAWEED OYSTER PLATE. $40.00-60.00. 10¼″ d. Probably American.

BANKS AND THORLEY FERN AND BOW PLATE. $55.00-75.00. 8" d. English registry mark. This concern located in Hanley, registered the design on April 10, 1883 with patent #396648.

ETRUSCAN CAULIFLOWER PLATE. $85.00-110.00. 9" d. These were also made in a 6" ($55.00-65.00) and a 7" ($65.00-75.00) size.

WEDGWOOD LOBSTER AND VEGETABLES PLATE. $135.00-155.00. 8¾" d. Impressed Wedgwood.

TRENTON-TYPE BIRD PLATE. $75.00-95.00. 8¼" d. Attributed to the Eureka Pottery Co., Trenton, NJ.

WEDGWOOD ORIENTAL PLATTER. $110.00-135.00. 13″ l. approx. This pattern was also done in a plate with a turquoise background.

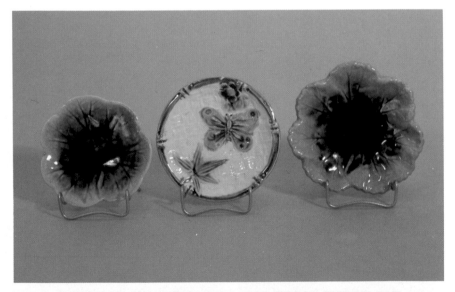

R. to L. ETRUSCAN GERANIUM LEAF "OLD STYLE" BUTTER PAT. $35.00-45.00. All approx. 3″ d. This older version of the Etruscan geranium leaf is much thicker and has a distinct "ruffled" effect which the later version lacks. FIELDING BUTTERFLY BUTTERPAT. $18.00-28.00. Impressed Fielding mark. ETRUSCAN "LATER-STYLE" GERANIUM BUTTER PAT. $18.00-28.00.

WEDGWOOD DOLPHIN OYSTER
PLATE. $95.00-125.00. 9¼″ d. Im-
pressed Wedgwood with the English
registry mark.

WATER LILY COBALT CENTERED
PLATE. $35.00-45.00. 8″ d. approx. A
nice rendition of the water lily pattern with a more naturalistic style
than usually seen on plates of this
type.

BANKS AND THORLEY BAMBOO
AND BASKETWEAVE PLATE.
$35.00-45.00. 7¾″ d. Also a tall coffee
pot, tea kettle, teacup with butterfly
handle, basket, and pitchers and
syrup pitchers among others.
Unmarked.

BLACKBERRY AND BASKETWEAVE
PLATE. $65.00-85.00. 10½″ d. Unusual
for its large size and turquoise
background. Most commonly found
in a smaller size with a white
background.

BEGONIA CENTERED "EAT THY BREAD WITH THANKFULNESS" BREAD TRAY. $95.00-145.00. 13″ l. The motto is in raised letters around the border. These "motto bread trays" form a distinct collecting category.

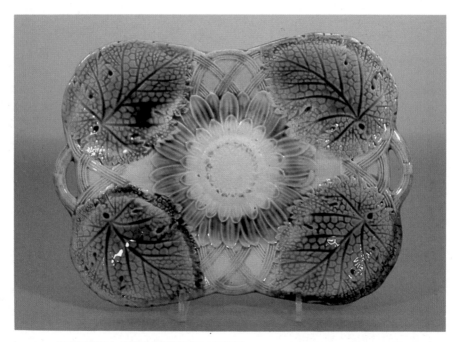

BEGONIA CORNERED PLATTER. $85.00-110.00. Approx. 11″ l.

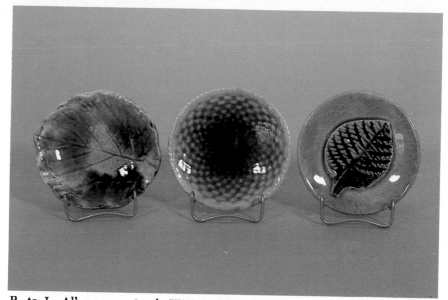

R. to L. All approx. 3" d. TWO-TONED LEAF BUTTERPAT. $12.00-18.00.
ETRUSCAN WICKER BUTTERPAT. $18.00-28.00. LEAF SHAPED BUTTER
PAT. $12.00-18.00.

WILD ROSE PLATTER WITH EYELET HANDLES. $65.00-85.00.

ETRUSCAN BEGONIA LEAF TRAY. $35.00-50.00. 9″ l. Also produced in an 8″ version. Coloration varies. These were originally intended as pickle dishes.

SHELL, SEAWEED AND OCEAN WAVES PLATTER. $145.00-175.00. 13½″ l.

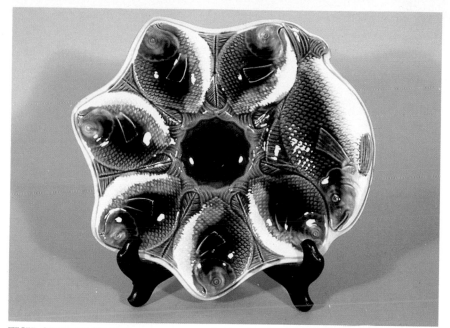

FISH OYSTER PLATE. $110.00-145.00. 10" d. Also in another version without the large fish.

ETRUSCAN CONVENTIONAL TEAPOT STAND. $210.00-250.00. 7" d. Small protrusions on the back hold this up off the table. Very rare.

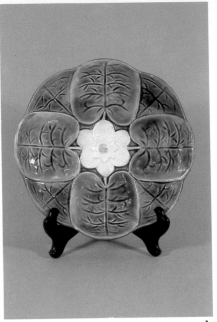

MULTI-COLOR SHELL OYSTER PLATE. $110.00-145.00. 10″ d. approx.

POND LILY PLATE. $45.00-55.00. 9″ d.

SQUARE FLORAL PIN TRAY. $18.00-25.00. 5¼″ d.

STRAWBERRY BLOSSOMS PLATE. $65.00-75.00. 8″ d. Probably George Jones.

HALF-MOON SEAWEED OYSTER PLATE. $110.00-145.00. 8" d. approx.

LEAF AND FLORAL OVAL PLATTER. $145.00-185.00. 15" l.

MINTON BASKETWEAVE AND SEAWEED OYSTER PLATE. $200.00-225.00.
9″ l. Impressed Minton.

R. to L. ETRUSCAN WICKER AND BEGONIA BUTTER PAT. $25.00-30.00. 3″ d.
ETRUSCAN SUNFLOWER UNDERPLATE. $125.00-150.00. 5″ d. ETRUSCAN
BEGONIA LEAF BUTTER PAT. $25.00-30.00. 3¾″ l.

BIRD AND FAN OVAL PLATTER. $145.00-185.00. 14″ l.

MOTTLED CENTER OVAL PLATTER. $125.00-165.00. 14″ l.

R. to L. ETRUSCAN LEAF ON PLATE BUTTER PAT. $25.00-30.00. 3″ d.
WEDGWOOD ASTOR BUTTERPAT. $20.00-25.00. 3″ d. WEDGWOOD SHELL
AND SEAWEED BUTTER PAT. $25.00-30.00. 3″ d.

HOLDCROFT RECTANGULAR PLATTER. $125.00-150.00. 13½″ l. Impressed J.
Holdcroft.

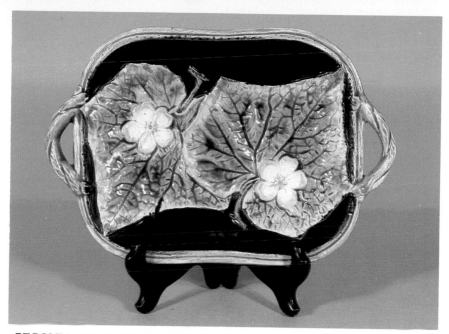

BEGONIA AND FLORAL OPEN HANDLED PLATTER. $110.00-135.00. 11½″ l.

FLORAL BORDERED PLATE. $75.00-110.00. 9″ d. Probably George Jones.

MOTTLED CENTER RASBERRY PATTERN PLATTER. $75.00-110.00. 11¾" l.

POND LILY BREAD TRAY. $125.00-150.00. 13" l.

WEDGWOOD CHRYSANTHEMUM PLATE. $85.00-125.00. 9" d. Impressed Wedgwood.

OVAL FERN, FLORAL AND BOW PLATTER. $110.00-135.00. 14" l. Attributed to Banks & Thorley, Hanley, England.

ETRUSCAN BEGONIA PLATE. $85.00-110.00. 9″ d.

BANKS AND THORLEY CAKE PLATE. $65.00-95.00. 10″ d.

CLIFTON DECOR BLACKBERRY PLATTER. $110.00-145.00. 13″ d. Clifton Decor mark. See mark No. 11.

OVAL FAN AND BUTTERFLY PLATTER. $135.00-165.00. 13¼″ l. Impressed shield mark.

COBALT CENTERED PICKET FENCE PLATTER. $125.00-145.00. 14″ l.

BIRD IN FLIGHT TURQUOISE PLATE. $85.00-110.00. 8½″ d. Attributed to J. Holdcroft.

"EAT THY BREAD WITH THANKFULNESS" WHEAT PATTERN BREAD TRAY. $125.00-150.00. 13″ l.

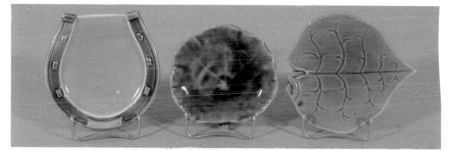

R. to L. All approx. 3″ d. GREEN LEAF BUTTER PAT. $15.00-18.00. WEDGWOOD GREEN LEAF BUTTER PAT. $18.00-22.00. Impressed Wedgwood. WEDGWOOD HORSESHOE BUTTER PAT. $25.00-35.00, Impressed Wedgwood.

R. to L. FLORAL BUTTER PAT. $15.00-20.00. All approx. 3″ d. WEDGWOOD SHELL AND SEAWEED BUTTER PAT. $25.00-30.00. THREE GREEN LEAF BUTTER PAT. $15.00-18.00.

HOLDCROFT BASKETWEAVE AND FLORAL PLATE. $85.00-110.00. 9" d. Impressed JH monogram. See mark No. 5.

CIRCULAR BANANA LEAF PLATTER. $110.00-135.00. 12" d.

PINEAPPLE PLATE. $95.00-120.00. 9" d.

TEA SERVICE

BLUE FLORAL SUGAR AND CREAM PITCHER. $55.00-75.00 pair. R. to L. 3″ h. 4″ h.

BIRD SUGAR AND CREAM PITCHER. $65.00-85.00. R. to L. 2¼″ h. 3½″ h.

DRUM SHAPED TWIG FOOTED TEA SET. $250.00-350.00. R. to L. 3¾″ h. 6½″ h. 6″ h.

STRAWBERRY AND BOW TEAPOT. $150.00-185.00. 6″ h. A strawberry on the finial and on the handle, this pattern was also done in a platter and dessert plates.

FLORAL SUGAR AND CREAM PITCHER. $55.00-75.00 pair. R. to L. 3″ h. 3½″ h.

WATER LILY TEAPOT. $95.00-110.00. 4″ h. approx. Part of a large family of the water lily pattern.

FLORAL SUGAR AND CREAM PITCHER. $55.00-75.00 pair.

PYRAMID TEASET. $135.00-165.00 if all pieces present. 6½" h. approx. teapot. 3½" h. approx. creamer. Sugar is missing lid here. These timely pieces were made to commemorate the obelisk in central park, New York City.

TURQUOISE BASKETWEAVE AND FLORAL 3 PIECE TEASET. $165.00-195.00. R. to L. 3½" h. 6" h. 4½" h.

WARDLE'S FERN AND BAMBOO CUP AND SAUCER AND SUGAR BOWL. R. to L. $85.00-110.00. $65.00-95.00. Produced by Wardle & Co. of Hanley, these bear the English registry mark and are part of a large series of pieces.

TREE BARK AND FOOTED THREE PIECE TEASET. $175.00-225.00. R. to L. 3"
h. 6½" h. 4½" h. Also look for a pitcher in this pattern. Nicely detailed spout in
the form of a tree branch. Intricately shaped finial.

ETRUSCAN BIRD AND IRIS THREE PIECE TEASET. $400.00-600.00 if all
pieces match. L. to R. 5" h. 6" h. 3¾" h. The lid to the teapot here is not the cor-
rect color. Scarce. Also with a blue background.

ROSE AND ROPE THREE PIECE TEASET AND PLATTER. Platter 15½″ l. $110.00-145.00. Teaset $145.00-185.00. R. to L. 3½″ h. 6″ h. 4½″ h. This pattern was also done in plates and compotes.

ETRUSCAN BAMBOO TEASET AND PLATE. Plate $75.00-95.00. 8″ d. R. to L. Spooner (rare) $110.00-125.00. 4¼″ h. Cream Pitcher $85.00-95.00. 4½″ h. Teapot $165.00-195.00. 6¾″ h. Sugar Bowl $110.00-125.00. 6″ h. One of the "Big Three" patterns produced by Griffin, Smith, and Hill (others are Shell and Seaweed and Cauliflower), this was made in a full tea set including waste bowl and covered butter dish. Only one size plate was produced.

BIRD AND FAN COBALT SUGAR
BOWL. $95.00-110.00. 4½" h. Pro-
duced in a teaset, also with a yellow
background.

FLORAL CUP AND SAUCER. $85.00-
110.00. 5¼" d. saucer.

SEASHELL AND OCEAN WAVES
CREAM PITCHER. $55.00-65.00. 4" h.
Belongs to a large family of shell and
wave pieces.

BAMBOO AND FLORAL CUP AND
SAUCER. $85.00-110.00. 6" d. saucer
approx.

ETRUSCAN SHELL AND SEAWEED CREAM PITCHER AND SUGAR BOWL.
R. to L. $110.00-145.00. 3½" h. $150.00-175.00. 5" h. This is the cream pitcher to
the coffee set. There is one size smaller which goes with the tea set. The double
handled covered sugar bowl is rare.

FIELDING FAN CUP AND SAUCER.
$110.00-125.00. 7" d. saucer. The cup
has the English registry mark and the
saucer is impressed FIELDING. Also
in a smaller version.

WEDGWOOD SHELL AND
SEAWEED TEAPOT. $325.00-425.00.
7" h.

ETRUSCAN SHELL AND SEAWEED CUP AND SAUCER, COFFEE POT, TEA POT, AND PLATES. R. to L. Tea cup and saucer. $110.00-155.00. 6″ d. saucer. Coffee Pot. $225.00-295.00. 6¼″ h. Teapot. $215.00-285.00. 6″ h. Plate. $145.00-165.00. 9″ d. (rare). Plate. $85.00-110.00. 8″ d. There is also a coffee sized cup and saucer with a 7″ d. saucer which is more scarce than the teacup size. $125.00-165.00. Beware of coffee cups with teacup (6″ d.) saucers!

FLYING CRANE TEAPOT. $125.00-150.00. 6¾″ h.

PINEAPPLE CUP AND SAUCER AND SUGAR BOWL. R. to L. $75.00-95.00.
5½" d. $85.00-145.00. 4¾" d.

BOW AND LEAF CREAM PITCHER. $55.00-65.00. 3¼" h. English Registry
mark.

WATER LILY COFFEE CUP AND SAUCER. $95.00-110.00. 6½″ d. saucer.

CHICK ON NEST TEAPOT. $125.00-145.00. 6″ h. approx. The little chick forms the finial while the teapot is a twig and leaf entwined nest.

SHELL AND SEAWEED SUGAR BOWL WITH FISH FINIAL AND HANDLES. $150.00-175.00. 5" h. approx. High level of craftsmanship and design.

BASKETWEAVE AND FLORAL TEAPOT AND SUGAR BOWL. R. to L. $55.00-75.00. 4" h. $110.00-145.00. 6" h. approx.

COBALT BIRD TEAPOT. $200.00-250.00. 6¾″ h. This unusual teapot has a long necked bird on each side. On the spout, one side has a bird and the other a butterfly. Similar in design to the Etruscan bird teapot, this example shows a design refinement — when tea is served from the Etruscan teapot it spills out between the body and the lid. The lid on this teapot is only a small rectangular section under the handle — the tea stays in!

ETRUSCAN ALBINO SHELL AND SEAWEED SPOONER AND CREAM PITCHER. L. to R. $85.00-120.00. 3¼″ h. $95.00-130.00. 3½″ h. Unmarked. Only about one in ten albino pieces bears the Etruscan Majolica mark.

FIELDING HUMMINGBIRD COF-
FEEPOT. $225.00-275.00. 9″ h. English
Registry mark. Also in a pitcher.

DRUM SHAPED TEAPOT. $150.00-
175.00. 9″ h.

SAMUEL LEAR SUNFLOWER AND
CLASSICAL URN MUSTACHE CUP
AND SAUCER. $175.00-225.00, 6½″ d.
saucer. Samuel Lear of Hanley,
England registered this design on
August 27, 1881, patent #369202. Also
in plates, platters, and cakestands.

PARROT ON A BRANCH SUGAR
BOWL. $95.00-125.00. 5½″ h.

ETRUSCAN ALBINO TEAPOT AND SUGAR BOWL. R. to L. $150.00-175.00. 5″ h. $200.00-250.00. 5½″ h. Only the sugar bowl bears the circular Etruscan Majolica mark.

MELON WITH BUMPS TEAPOT. $195.00-225.00. 6½″ h. Also in a cream colored background.

CORN TEAPOT AND SUGAR BOWL. R. to L. $175.00-225.00. 6½" h. $150.00-175.00. 6" h. Most beautiful and rare!

FIELDING SHELL CREAM PITCHER AND SUGAR BOWL. L. to R. $100.00-125.00. $85.00-110.00. 4" h. approx. 5" h. approx. English registry mark. Impressed FIELDING.

PEWTER TOPPED TEAPOT. $150.00-195.00. 6″ h. The pewter top adds value.

VASES

BIRD IN FLIGHT AND POND LILY
VASE. $125.00-145.00. 10" h. approx.
Also comes in a cobalt background.

PINEAPPLE HAND VASE. $185.00-
225.00. 7¼" h. Very rare Victorian od
dity. The hand even sports a cuff with
tassel! Rare.

FOOTED BIRD VASE. $200.00-250.00.
7" h. Magnificent workmanship
detail, and coloring. Probably produced by one of the major English
potters — possibly Copeland or
Minton.

LION FOOTED COBALT VASE.
$110.00-135.00. 9″ h.

SCALLOPED TOP FERN VASE.
$195.00-225.00. 9½″ d. Possibly
George Jones.

ETRUSCAN CELERY VASE. $350.00-
450.00. 8¾″ h. One of the most lovely
of the Griffin, Smith, and Hill pieces
and very, very rare.

PAIR OF GIRL AND BOY CANDLESTICKS. $125.00-155.00 pr. 7" h. Probably French.

MINTON ASPARAGUS SERVER. $350.00-395.00. 10¼" l. 8¾" w. Impressed MINTON.

DEERHEAD CIGARETTE HOLDER.
$75.00-110.00. 5″ h.

POND LILY JARDINAIRE. $150.00-
195.00. 8″ h.

STRAWBERRY SERVER WITH IN-
DIVIDUAL SUGAR BOWL AND
CREAM PITCHER. $250.00-325.00.
10¼″ l. 8″ w. These are rare and
desirable pieces particularly with the
separate sugar bowl and cream pitcher intact. They fit into the circular
wells in the server. Almost exactly
like the Etruscan strawberry server,
although this example is unmarked.

CONCH SHELL ON FIGURAL CORAL. $120.00-145.00. 4″ h.

WEDGWOOD CREAM BOAT, OPEN SUGAR BOWL AND STRAWBERRY SERVING DISHES. $150.00-165.00 cream boat. 3″ h. $150.00-165.00 open sugar bowl. 3″ h. $75.00-95.00. 6¾″ d. each strawberry serving dish.

ASPARAGUS SERVER ON OCEAN WAVES. $225.00-250.00. 11" l.

FIGURAL DEER'S HEAD SWEETMEAT SERVER. $225.00-250.00 4½" h. Most beautiful with very excellent workmanship. Possibly Copeland.

STANDING MONKEY WEARING
LOINCLOTH MATCH HOLDER.
$125.00-150.00. 7¾" h.

FAN CUSPIDOR. $200.00-225.00. 6½"
h.

BOY RIDING A DOLPHIN POND LI-
LY CENTERPIECE. $275.00-350.00.
12" h. White central lily flower sur-
rounded by large green lily pad.
Beautiful from any angle.

ELEPHANT MATCH HOLDER.
$195.00-250.00. 8" h. Probably English.

ETRUSCAN SUNFLOWER CUSPIDOR. $250.00-300.00. 6″ h. Very rare.

SHELL AND SEAWEED CUSPIDOR. $145.00-175.00. 6″ h.

FLORAL CUSPIDOR. $125.00-165.00. 5½" h.

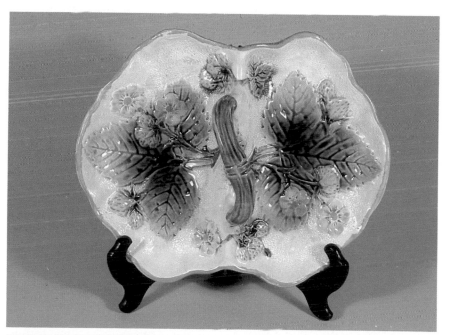

RUSTIC HANDLED SERVER. $145.00-185.00. 10½" l. Decorated with strawberries, leaves, and blossoms. A perfect example of the motif suggesting the intended use.

THOMAS SHIRLEY LEOPARD FROG HANDLED URN. $195.00-250.00. 7″ h.
Impressed TS underneath the base. Earlier than true Victorian majolica this
piece dates c. 1850.

MARKS

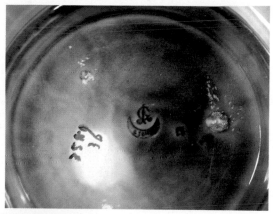

1. GEORGE JONES & SONS.
Stoke, England. c. 1864-1907
"& Sons" was added to the GJ
monogram in 1873.

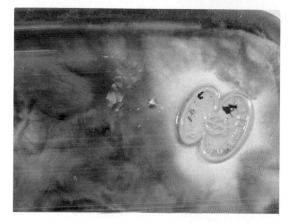

2. GEORGE JONES. This
mark is on an applied pad.

3. GEORGE JONES. This
mark is probably earlier
than either of the others. The
diamond shaped figure is the
English Registry mark.

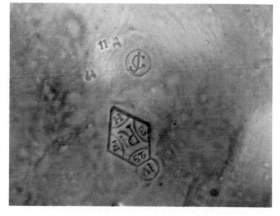

4. JOSEPH HOLDCROFT.
Longton, England. c.
1865-1906.

5. JOSEPH HOLDCROFT.
Impressed monogram.

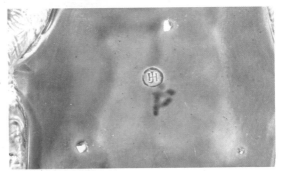

6. S. FIELDING & CO. (LTD.)
Stoke, England. c. 1879-. The
name "FIELDING" was im-
pressed in a straight line
either with or without the
diamond shaped English
registry mark shown here.

7. W. T. COPELAND (&
SONS LTD.). Stoke, England.
c. 1847-. Impressed
"COPELAND" along with
the English registry mark
and the name "GILL" which
may have been the importer
on this particular piece.

8. WORCESTER ROYAL PORCELAIN COMPANY LTD. Worcester, England. c. 1862-. Impressed crown over circle.

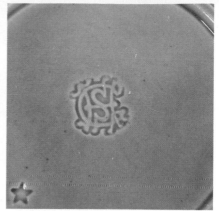

10. GRIFFIN, SMITH AND HILL. The GSH monogram without the encircling phrase "Etruscan Majolica" as above is considered to be the earlier mark. This mark is always used inside the pedestal on footed pieces, on butter pats, as well as many other pieces.

9. GRIFFIN, SMITH AND HILL. Phoenixville, PA. 1879-1889.

11. CHESAPEAKE POTTERY. Baltimore, MD. c. 1880.

12. WELLSVILLE CHINA CO. Wellsville, OH. c. 1879.

13. EDWIN BENNETT POTTERY CO. Baltimore, MD. c. 1873.

BIBLIOGRAPHY

Barber, Edwin Atlee. The Pottery and Porcelain of the United States and Marks of American Potters. Feingold & Lewis, 1976.

Cushion, J. P. Pocket Book of British Ceramic Marks. Alden Press, Oxford. 1979.

Godden, Geoffrey A. British Pottery, An Illustrated Guide. Clarkson N. Potter, Inc, New York, 1975.

Godden, Geoffrey A. British Pottery and Porcelain. Bonanza Books, New York, 1964.

Godden, Geoffrey A. Encyclopedia of British Pottery and Porcelain Marks. Bonanza Books, New York, 1964.

James, Arthur E. The Potters and Potteries of Chester County, Pennsylvania. Schiffer Publishing Co., Exton, PA., 1978.

Rebert, M. Charles. American Majolica 1850-1900, Wallace-Homestead Book Company, Des Moines, Iowa 1981.

Rickerson, Wildey C. Majolica, Collect it for Fun and Profit, Pequot Press, Chester, Ct., 1972.

Time Life, Encyclopedia of Collectibles. Time Life Books, Alexandria, Virginia, 1979.